TECHNOLOGY IN TIMES PAST

Aztec, Inca, and Maya

ROBERT SNEDDEN

A⁺

Smart Apple Media

Smart Apple Media is published by Black Rabbit Books
P.O. Box 3263, Mankato, Minnesota 56002

Printed in China

Library of Congress Cataloging-in-Publication Data

Snedden, Robert.
    Aztec, Inca, and Maya / Robert Snedden.
    p. cm.—(Smart Apple Media. Technology in times past)
    Includes index.
    Summary: "Covers the inventions and technology of the Aztecs, Incas, and Maya and how their ideas influenced technology today"—Provided by publisher.
    ISBN 978-1-59920-299-0
    1. Inventions—Central America—History—Juvenile literature. 2. Technology—Central America—History—Juvenile literature. 3. Inventions—Mexico—History—Juvenile literature. 4. Technology—Mexico— History—Juvenile literature. 5. Aztecs—Material culture—Juvenile literature. 6. Incas—Material culture—Juvenile literature. 7. Mayas—Material culture—Juvenile literature. I. Title.
T24.A1S64 2009
609.72—dc22

                                                          2008000447

Designed by Helen James
Edited by Pip Morgan
Illustrations by Graham Rosewarne
Picture research by Su Alexander

Picture acknowledgements
Page 7t Marco Cristofori/Corbis, b Vanni Archive/Corbis; 8 Guenter Rossenbach/Zefa/ Corbis; 9 Arcaid/Corbis; 10 Massimo Listri/Corbis; 11 Mimmo Jodice/Corbis; 13t Guenter Rossenbach/Zefa/Corbis, b Bill Ross/Corbis; 14 Bettmann/Corbis; 15 Mimmo Jodice/Corbis; 16 Araldo de Luca/Corbis; 17 Morley von Sternberg/Arcaid/Corbis; 18 Free Agents Ltd/ Corbis; 21t Jose Fuste Raga/Zefa/Corbis, b Sandro Vannini/Corbis; 22 Erich Lessing/AKG Images; 23 Fine Art Photographic Library/Corbis; 25t Adam Woolfitt/Corbis, b Richard Cummins/Corbis, 26 Erich Lessing/AKG Images; 27 Richard Hamilton Smith/Corbis; 28 Eye Ubiquitous/Corbis; 29 Museo Della Civilta Romana Rome/ Gianni Dagli Orti/The Art Archive; 30 Araldo de Luca/Corbis; 31 Bruce Adams; Eye Ubiquitous/Corbis; 33t Joseph Martin/AKG Images, b Anders Ryman/Corbis; 34 Araldo de Luca/Corbis; 35 Museo Della Civilta Romana Rome/Gianni Dagli Orti/The Art Archive; 36 Araldo de Luca/Corbis; 37t James L. Amos/Corbis, b Macduff Everton/Corbis; 38 Erich Lessing/AKG Images; 39 Owen Franken/Corbis

Front cover Massimo Listri/Corbis

9 8 7 6 5 4 3 2 1

CONTENTS

THE NEW WORLD

When Spanish explorers first reached the Americas in the sixteenth century, they thought they had discovered a New World. They were surprised to find that this new land was a large continent already occupied by people, such as the Aztecs, Inca, and Maya, who were part of great civilizations.

MESOAMERICA

The region that includes Mexico and Central America is called Mesoamerica, which means "Middle America." There, several civilizations had risen and fallen before Europeans knew it existed. One belonged to the Olmec people, who flourished between 1200 and 400 B.C. Another was the mighty Teotihuácan, who were at the height of their power from A.D. 150 to 450 and who built the largest city in the Americas at the time.

At the start of the sixteenth century, the dominant civilizations of Mesoamerica were the Maya and the Aztecs. The kingdom of the Maya had begun around 1000 B.C. It did not have a capital city or a single ruler. Each Mayan city was self-governing, like the city-states of ancient Greece. The Maya were most powerful from around A.D. 300 to 900. There are still about six million Mayans living in Central America today, mainly in Mexico. Around A.D. 1200, the Mexican people rose to

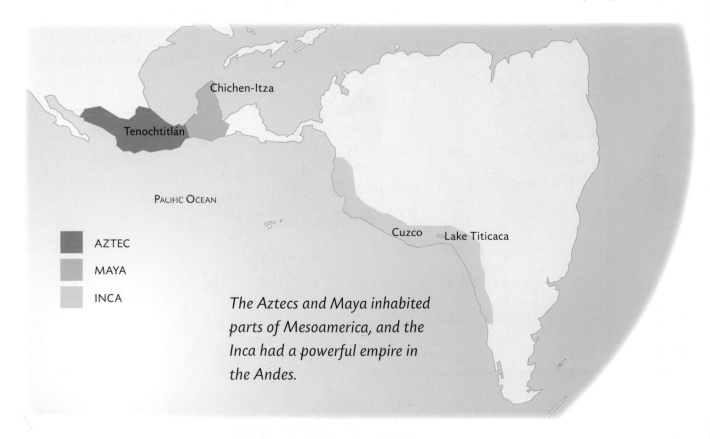

The Aztecs and Maya inhabited parts of Mesoamerica, and the Inca had a powerful empire in the Andes.

Chichen-Itza

Tenochtitlán

PACIFIC OCEAN

Cuzco   Lake Titicaca

AZTEC

MAYA

INCA

The Inca city of Machu Picchu attracts many visitors to its remote location in the Andes.

power and built a strong civilization, forging alliances and waging war to extend their control. We know them as the Aztecs.

THE ANDES

The Andes is one of the world's greatest mountain ranges, stretching like a backbone along the length of South America. People have probably lived here for more than 13,000 years. They discovered how to work with gold, silver, and copper, and used these metals to make tools and jewelry.

A number of different peoples fought for power in the region, including the Huari, who dominated much of what is now Peru from around A.D. 500 to 1200. The Huari people

The Maya made many clay figures that were placed beside a body when it was buried.

introduced an agricultural system of terraced fields that helped them to grow more food in the mountains.

In 1438, the Inca people conquered the area around Cuzco, which they made their capital city. They became the dominant civilization in the region, but the Spaniards ended their power a hundred years later.

The civilizations of the Andes and Mesoamerica built magnificent cities, developed their own way of looking at life, and created great works of art and learning.

BUILDING HOMES

The Aztecs, Inca, and Maya built their homes with local materials. Aztec and Maya homes were usually made of mud brick, while the Inca also used stone. The roofs of the houses were thatched with reeds or grasses. Mostly, the houses had just one room with only a little furniture.

Today, Mayan people continue to live in homes built in the traditional style.

AZTEC HOMES

The Aztecs built their homes from adobe, which is a mixture of sun-dried mud and straw, and covered them with a thatched roof. The word "adobe" is Spanish for "dried brick." Aztec homes were open plan, which means they had one big room divided into areas for different activities. There was an inside courtyard with a kitchen area for preparing food, an eating area where the whole family shared a meal, a sleeping area where everyone rested together, and a small family shrine with statues of gods displayed on a table.

INCA HOMES

The Inca people, who lived on the Pacific coast of northwestern South America, also built adobe houses. The roofs were flat and the walls were covered in painted plaster for extra protection.

In mountain towns, a typical Inca home was built of stone. In towns, several homes were built together around a central courtyard. Timber beams attached to stone pegs ran across the top of the house, supporting a roof frame that was covered in thatch. Most houses were single story, although a few had upper floors. If a house had a second story, it was reached by rope ladders inside the house or by stone steps outside.

The Inca did not spend much time indoors, so their homes had little furniture. Many houses had no windows or chimneys, so they must have been very dark and smoky inside.

The doors were not rectangular like ours; they were shaped like trapezoids. The top of the door was narrower than the bottom.

MAYAN HOMES

Many of the Maya who live in rural Mexico today have homes very similar to those built by their ancestors hundreds of years ago.

The walls of Mayan houses are built from woven sticks covered with a mixture of red soil, brush weeds, and water, called *embarro*. The roof is made of sloping palm leaves. Mayan houses have a front and back door, but they do not have any windows.

People make adobe bricks for their homes in present-day Peru.

CITIES OF THE INCA

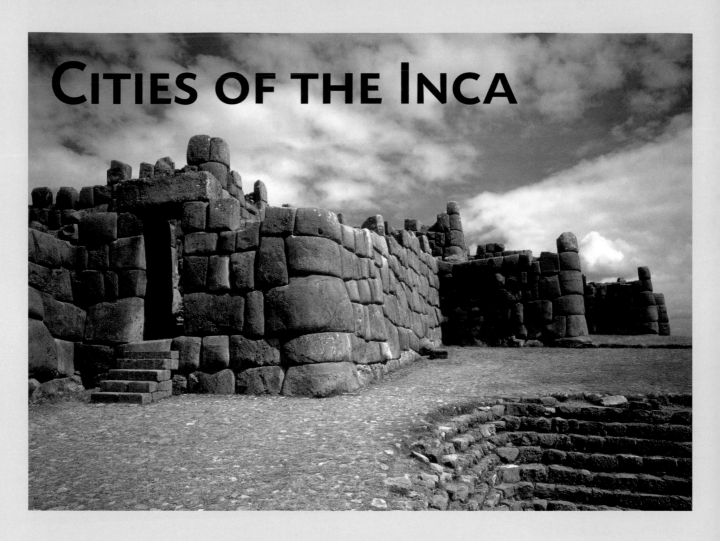

The Inca empire stretched from the Pacific coast to the mountains of the Andes. Inca cities were built from local materials. For example, Cuzco had many stone buildings, such as Sacsayhuaman, while Chan Chan on the coast had mud brick buildings laid out in a grid pattern of straight lines.

The remains of the Inca fortress of Sacsayhuaman stands in Cuzco, Peru.

CAPITAL CITY

The Inca made Cuzco the capital city of their empire. At the time of the Spanish conquest, it may have had around 200,000 inhabitants. Legend says that Cuzco was laid out in the shape of a puma, with the fortress of Sacsayhuaman as its head. The closely fitting stone walls of the fortress were 52 feet (16 m) high. The city was built so well that Cuzco has survived several earthquakes.

INCA MASONS

The Inca were famous for their masonry, or stonework. They cut, ground, and polished blocks of stone until the surface was smooth and perfectly shaped. The workmanship was superb and the stones fit together so precisely that no mortar was needed to hold them together. Their only tools were stone hammers and wet sand, which they used to polish the blocks.

MACHU PICCHU

Around 1450, the Inca built a city high in the Andes called Machu Picchu. The Spaniards never discovered it because it was so remote. It consisted of 143 granite buildings, including many temples and other important buildings. An irrigation system that supplied water fountains may have also carried water into people's homes.

TWO TYPES OF MASONRY

The skilled Inca stonemasons used two types of masonry for their stone buildings—coursed masonry and polygonal masonry.

They used coursed masonry for constructing the walls of important buildings such as palaces and temples. In coursed masonry, all the stones were carefully cut into rectangular shapes and were placed in flat, smooth, and horizontal rows. The stones for the higher parts of the wall were smaller than those at the bottom. This made the building look balanced and pleasing to the eye.

The Inca used polygonal masonry to build the homes of ordinary people. This involved finding stones of different shapes and carefully fitting them together like the pieces of a jigsaw puzzle.

The walls in this street (above) in Cuzco, Peru, were once part of an Inca palace.

The stones in this drystone wall were connected by polygonal masonry.

11

CITIES OF MESOAMERICA

The landscape of Mesoamerica ranges from jungle highlands to coastal plains. The Maya built their cities in both highlands and lowlands, whereas the Aztecs built theirs in the highlands. The central areas of Mesoamerican cities were reserved for the palaces of the rulers and for public buildings and temples.

The Avenue of the Dead was the central street in the city of Teotihuácan.

ANCIENT CITY

The city of Teotihuácan is one of the most impressive cities in Mesoamerica. The ruins are about 25 miles (40 km) northeast of present-day Mexico City.

During the 1st and 2nd centuries A.D., Teotihuácan became the region's largest city, covering around 8 square miles (21 sq km) with around 80,000 inhabitants. By the fourth century, the city's influence had spread throughout Mesoamerica.

The city was divided by the Avenue of the Dead, which is more than 1.5 miles (2.4 km) long. Buildings were arranged, often symmetrically, on either side of the avenue. Many buildings in Teotihuácan had sloping sides and a flat rectangular top.

Later, the Maya adopted this architectural style, known as the *talud-tablero* style. Most Mayans lived in large apartment blocks that often also housed workshops for making pottery and other crafts.

Who built Teotihuácan remains a mystery. The Aztecs thought it was the Toltecs who were important in the region between the tenth and twelfth centuries A.D. But the city was founded before the Toltec civilization arose. Others think that the Totonac people built it, but there is no real evidence to support this. Some research suggests that Teotihuácan was a multicultural center, whose inhabitants came from many regions.

CITY OF CANALS

During the thirteenth century, the Aztecs arrived in the Valley of Mexico, led by their chief, Tenoch. They were a nomadic people who, according to their legends, had come from a place called Aztlan in the north of Mexico. Finding the best land in the valley already occupied by rival peoples, they settled on two small swampy islands in Lake Texcoco. From a small settlement of reed and grass huts, the city of Tenochtitlán began to grow. The Aztecs developed the *chinampa* system

of farming that allowed them to reclaim land from the swamps (see page 16) and make it fertile and productive. People traveled along the city's many canals, while causeways linked the city to the mainland and allowed smaller communities to grow. By 1519, there were around 400,000 people living in and around Tenochtitlan, making it the largest population center in Mesoamerica. Today, Mexico City stands on the site of Tenochtitlan.

THE BALL GAME

A sport called the ball game was played throughout Mesoamerica. The goal was to put a rubber ball through stone rings at the opponent's end of the court. Every city had a ballcourt. The largest, at Chichen Itza, was 607 feet (185 m) long and 223 feet (68 m) wide. The Maya saw the game as a battle between the people of Earth and the forces of the underworld, while the Aztecs saw it as a fight between the moon and the sun. The game was violent and sometimes a player died.

The remains of a Mayan ball game court have been found at Uxmal, Mexico.

THE PYRAMIDS OF MESOAMERICA

The Aztec and Maya built pyramids in their cities in Mesoamerica. Apart from the Egyptians, no other civilization has built such structures on a large scale. The Egyptians built pyramids as tombs for their rulers, but the Mesoamerican pyramids were temples to the gods.

The temple pyramid of Kukulkan stands at Chichen Itza in Mexico.

STEPPED PYRAMIDS

Unlike smooth-sided Egyptian pyramids, Mesoamerican pyramids usually had steps on one or more sides leading up to a temple on the top. Some pyramids were so steep that the top couldn't be seen from ground level.

The Maya often built astronomical observatories as well as temples at the top of their pyramids. The temple pyramid of Kukulkan in the Mayan city of Chichen Itza

was built so that priests could study the stars in the heavens. It has four staircases of 91 steps, one on each side. Together with the platform on the top this makes 365, the number of days in a year.

On the days of the spring and autumn equinoxes, when the days and nights are the same length, the main stairway of the pyramid casts a shadow that looks like the body of a serpent. As the sun moves across the sky, the shadow moves down the pyramid to line up with a huge serpent's head carved in stone at the foot of the steps. The Maya believe this represents the god Quetzalcoatl, the Feathered Serpent, who was important throughout Mesoamerica as a god of creation and a giver of life.

THE CHIRPING PYRAMID

The temple pyramid of Kukulkan is remarkable in another way. If you stand at the foot of the pyramid and clap your hands together, the echo that comes back sounds remarkably like the chirp of the quetzal, a bird that is sacred to the Maya. Many archaeologists believe that the Maya designed the pyramid to produce this acoustic effect.

THE GREAT PYRAMID

The Great Pyramid of Cholula in Mexico is considered to be the largest monument in the world. It was built as a temple to the god

MOVING BLOCKS

The Maya, the Aztecs, and the Inca had no wheeled vehicles or pulleys. How they managed to move the enormous blocks of stone they used for building remains a mystery. We also have little idea how they raised the blocks into position. Perhaps they built ramps as the Egyptians did: once hundreds of men had dragged the stones up and put them into position, the ramps were removed.

Quetzalcoatl and has been added to by many generations of many peoples, from the second century B.C. up to the early sixteenth century A.D. Archaeologists have discovered more than 5 miles (8 km) of tunnels inside.

A carving of the feathered head of the god Quetzalcoatl has been found at the city of Teotihuácan.

Farming

Farming was very important to the thriving populations of the Aztec and Inca empires. The people of the Andes and Mesoamerica had a simple but nutritious diet, and maize and different varieties of beans were important crops. The Aztec and Maya grew tomatoes and avocados, while the Inca had many kinds of potatoes.

Aztec farmers had no plows or work animals such as oxen and horses, so they relied on their own muscle power. The Incas had llamas, but these animals were not strong enough to carry heavy loads.

Canals and Mounds

Often, the land was poor or difficult to work, so farmers invented ways to get the most from the soil. The Aztecs developed a unique system of farming where they reclaimed land from swamps and shallow lakes by making *chinampas*. The farmers, or *chinamperos*, dug out canals in the swamp, piling up the scooped-out earth on top of the reeds. In this way, they formed mounds, or *chinampas*, that were bordered on at least three sides by canals. Here, the farmers grew their crops.

Each *chinampa* was a few yards across and around 100 to 130 feet (30–40 m) long. Posts, or woven vines and branches, stabilized the sides of each *chinampa*. Often, willow trees were planted along the edges to help prevent erosion of the soil. The willows were also used for firewood and for building.

Workers tend a chinampa *in Xochimilco at the southern end of Mexico City.*

CREATING TERRACES

Farming on the side of a mountain is hard because rainwater washes the soil away. The Inca solved this problem by building terraces. They created a number of giant steps up the side of a hill or mountain, and hauled soil up in baskets from the plains below. All their hard work was rewarded by the increased yield in the crops that were grown on the terraces. Inca terraces were so successful that they are still used in the Andes today.

Crops are grown on terraces in mountain farms in a highland valley in the Andes.

Maize was a very important crop for the people of Mesoamerica and the Andes.

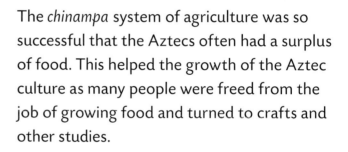

The *chinampa* system of agriculture was so successful that the Aztecs often had a surplus of food. This helped the growth of the Aztec culture as many people were freed from the job of growing food and turned to crafts and other studies.

GROWING SEEDS

The *chinamperos* started growing their plants in nurseries, which were located at one end of the *chinampa* beside a canal. They spread a thick layer of mud over a bed of waterweeds and then cut the land into blocks called *chapines* when it had set.

The *chinampero* made a hole in each *chapine*, dropped in a seed, then covered it with manure. The seeds were protected from frost by reeds and were well watered. When it was ready, the seedling was transplanted, still in its *chapine*, to a place on the *chinampa*, and covered with canal mud.

FOOD PREPARATION

The peoples of Mesoamerica and the Andes ate a variety of meat and fish. They hunted animals, such as wild pigs and deer, with bows and arrows and with clubs. In both regions, fishermen used harpoons, nets, and fishhooks made of bone or thorns to catch sea creatures.

POTATO VARIETIES

The potato plant is a native species of the Andes, which means it grows there naturally. Potatoes became a staple part of the Inca diet. The Inca grew around 200 different varieties of potatoes. A food that we take for granted today was unknown outside South America until the Spaniards brought potatoes back to Europe.

FREEZE-DRYING

The Inca developed very efficient ways of preserving, transporting, and storing food. They built and maintained food storehouses throughout the empire to supply the army wherever it went.

The Inca found a way of freeze-drying food. They left potatoes out at night to freeze in the low temperatures at high altitudes. During the day, when the temperature of the air rose, they trampled the potatoes under their feet, squeezing out the water, which then evaporated.

After a few days, they ended up with a dried potato product, known as *chuño*, which could be kept for more than a year if it was carefully stored. It was used to make *chuño* flour or added to soups and stews. The Inca used a similar process to freeze-dry meat to make *charqui*. Today, we make a dried beef snack called jerky, which gets its name from *charqui*.

A street vendor sells different varieties of potatoes at a market in Pisac, Peru.

A woman grinds maize with a large stone while she sits on the rushes of a floating island at Lake Titicaca, Peru.

Purepecha women in Mexico prepare tortillas and bake them over fires.

MOTHER MAIZE

The main cereal crop in both the Andes and Mesoamerica was maize. Maize is a particularly nutritious plant that grew well there and provided plenty of calories. It was so important to the people of the region that the Maya called it *kana*, which means "our mother."

TORTILLAS AND TAMALES

A common way of preparing maize was to mash it with a round grinding stone (called a mano) against a flat stone (called a metate) to make corn meal. This was mixed with water to make a dough for making tortillas, that was a staple part of the Aztec diet. The tortillas were cooked over a fire on a pottery disk called a comal. Both the Aztecs and Inca ate tamales, a sort of steamed maize wrap stuffed with vegetables and meat.

A VERSATILE PLANT

Another source of food for the Aztecs was the maguey plant, which is also known as the agave. It was a versatile plant because it had many uses. The Aztecs brewed the sap into a beer-like drink called pulque. They turned the thorns into needles and used the plant's fiber to weave rope.

19

Textiles and Clothing

The peoples of Mesoamerica and South America were skilled weavers who made textiles from plant fibers —mainly cotton, but also with fibers from yucca and agave plants. In the Andes, the Inca wove cloth from the wool of animals such as the alpaca, vicuña, and llama, as well as from cotton.

Spinning and Dyeing

The Inca spun fibers into yarn using a technique that has been used by people around the world. A weighted stick, called a hand spindle, was set spinning and the spinner teased out the fibers, winding them around the spindle as it turned to form the thread.

The yarn was dyed before it was woven into cloth. The Inca made dyes from a variety of plants and other natural sources. For example, grinding up cochineal beetles that are found on cactus plants made a red dye. It took about 70,000 beetles to make 1 pound (0.5 kg) of dye. The Inca made a purple dye from a shellfish found on the Pacific coast. This was similar to the imperial purple dye that was used by the emperors of ancient Rome.

The Backstrap Loom

The most common type of loom was the backstrap loom. People throughout the Americas used this simple but very effective piece of technology. The backstrap loom has two wooden poles called loom bars that hold the vertical warp threads. One bar is hung by a cord on a convenient tree or post.

A Maya woman from Guatemala weaves cloth using a backstrap loom.

An adjustable strap worn around the weaver's waist supports the other loom bar. The weaver keeps the yarn taut by leaning back against the strap.

Peruvians in traditional costume celebrate the festival of the First Inca, who landed on the shores of Lake Titicaca after descending from the sun.

Inca men wore a loincloth, sleeveless tunic and cloak, while women wore sleeveless dresses secured with waist sashes.

Aztecs and Inca of high status wore colorful, decorated clothes of the finest materials. The clothes of high-ranking Inca had geometric designs called *tocapus* woven into the cloth across the waistband.

WHAT PEOPLE WORE

The kind of clothes a person wore indicated his or her place, or status, in society. An ordinary Aztec man wore a loincloth and a cape that stopped above his knee. If he wore a cape that reached his ankles, he was committing an offense that was punishable by death! Aztec women wore skirts and tunics that they wrapped around themselves.

FEATHERWORKING

Featherworkers were some of the most skilled Aztec craftsmen. They made elaborate headdresses for warriors, priests, and other important people. The feathers were attached individually to a reed framework by tying them with thread and were often trimmed with precious stones, gold, and silver.

A drummer wears a traditional Aztec headdress with red and blue feathers.

Ceramics

The people of the Andes and Mesoamerica did not use a potter's wheel or a kiln. They made ceramics by shaping coils of clay by hand, by molding the clay, and by carving. Much of their pottery was plain and simple and intended for everyday use. They also made beautiful decorated ceramic pieces for religious ceremonies and for the wealthier members of society.

Aztec bowls decorated with images of skulls

Slipware

The people of Mesoamerica often produced a type of pottery called slipware. Pottery pieces were treated with a semi-liquid clay, called slip, before they were fired. Different colored slips were used to paint decorations on the pots. Glazes were very rarely used on the pottery.

One of their decorative techniques involved covering the shaped pot with wax or gum, which was then partly scraped away to leave a pattern. Next, the whole pot was covered in a pigment. When the pot was fired, the gum burned away, leaving only the areas that had been scraped free of gum with color.

Open Firing

The potters of the Americas did not use kilns to fire their pottery, as people did elsewhere in the world. Instead, they fired their pieces of pottery in an open fire or placed them in a pit in the ground over which a fire was built. Although they had no kilns, the potters still managed to create a type of pottery known as blackware. Usually, this is done by closing the kiln to prevent oxygen from reaching the pots during the firing process. The iron in the clay combines with other chemicals, turning the pot black or dark gray.

A stirrup-spouted vessel shaped like a monkey.

WHISTLING JARS

One of the more unusual types of pottery found in both Mesoamerica and the Andes is the whistling water jar. These jars were double vessels joined by hollow tubes through which water flowed from one to the other. As it did so, the water pushed air out of the vessel through a whistle. Some whistling jars were quite elaborate and made in the shape of animals, birds, or people. Some bird-shaped jars made bird-like burbling noises when they were tipped back and forth.

SOUTH AMERICAN POTTERY

The centers of pottery in South America were in present-day Bolivia and Peru. The Moche people in northern Peru made many pots that had stirrup spouts and depicted all kinds of themes.

The Inca usually produced their pottery to standard shapes, often using molds. One of the most typical of these designs is the *aryballos* jar. This had a conical base, so it probably had to be placed in some sort of stand. It also had two handles set low on the body and a flaring neck. Most Inca pottery was polished red, with geometric patterns in red, white, or black.

This Mayan bowl is decorated with the heads of three quetzal birds.

23

METALWORKING

Precious metals, such as gold, silver, and platinum, were worked 3,500 years ago in Peru. By the sixteenth century, the peoples of Mesoamerica and the Andes had developed a range of metalworking skills. They mainly used gold, silver, and copper, but also tin, lead, and platinum. They did not work with iron.

MINING AND PANNING

Metals came from mines that had narrow tunnels as deep as 130 feet (40 m), which followed a rich vein of metal. Metals were also washed from river gravel by panning. This was done by using digging sticks that were hardened by firing to break up the river bottom, and the loosened material was sifted in shallow trays. Sometimes the sifting revealed flecks of precious metals that had been washed down from the mountains.

NATIVE COPPER

Copper is one of the few metals that is found on its own—that is, not combined with another element. This is called native copper, and it does not need to be smelted to separate it from other compounds. It was used to make jewelry and tools for ordinary people.

This ornamental jaguar is made from native copper.

GOING FOR GOLD

Goldsmiths had a way of treating *tumbaga* to increase the amount of gold on the surface of the alloy, improving its appearance. They rubbed it with the juice of a plant, probably a type of wood sorrel. The juice contains oxalic acid, which dissolves the copper but leaves the gold untouched.

Andean people pan for gold today using similar techniques to their ancestors.

Native copper was also combined with gold to make *tumbaga,* an alloy that is harder than pure gold. The ratio of gold to copper varied widely. Some *tumbaga* was almost entirely gold, while some was almost entirely copper.

COLD WORKING

South American metalworkers were good at working with gold when it was cold. This is called cold working. They could also produce a vessel from a flat sheet of gold—a technique known as raising—and press the gold over molds to make a series of identical pieces.

The earliest known goldwork is almost 3,000 years old. It consists of embossed sheet gold decorations and was discovered in Chongoyape, Peru. Embossing is a method of decorating metals. Hammering and punching the back of the piece produces raised patterns on the surface of the metal.

Metalworkers in Ecuador made fine and elaborate beads from an alloy of gold and platinum. They did this by sintering, which is a technique that involves welding together small particles of metal by alternately hammering and heating—but without melting the metals. The Ecuadoreans used gold dust and small grains of platinum obtained from rivers.

CASTING METAL

The Moche people, who lived in northern Peru from about 200 B.C. to A.D. 600, were skilled metalworkers. They may have been the first to cast metal around A.D. 100. Casting involves pouring molten metal into a mold to produce a shape. The technique probably spread north and reached the civilizations of Mesoamerica in about A.D. 900.

WIND OVENS

The Inca smelted metals in clay furnaces that burned charcoal. They made holes in the front of the furnaces, and the wind increased the heat of the fire to make it hot enough to melt the metals. They placed these wind ovens, or *huaira*, on a windy hillside.

GOLD-PLATING

The Moche developed a way of gold-plating copper. They dissolved gold in a strong acid and placed a copper object in the liquid. The gold coated the object, which was removed and then heated to bind the gold permanently to the copper.

A gold ornament that the Aztecs wore on their lips

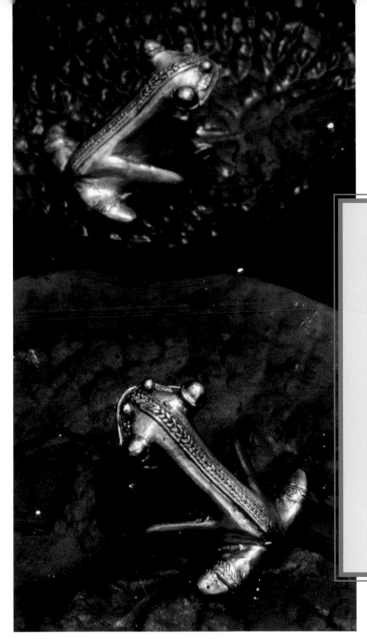

These ornamental frogs from Panama have been cast in gold.

SWEAT OF THE SUN, TEARS OF THE MOON

Gold and silver had great significance for the Inca people. They called gold "the sweat of the sun" and silver "the tears of the moon." Their gold and silver objects were used mostly for religious ceremonies and as jewelry for the rich and powerful. The Inca didn't need money. The people worked for the empire, and in turn, the empire supplied them with clothing and food.

AZTEC GOLD

Goldsmiths were among the most important men in Aztec society. The secrets of their craft were passed from father to son. They made intricate objects using the lost wax method of casting.

This method involved making a wax model of an object and covering it with clay. The clay was fired to harden it, and the melted wax was removed, leaving a hollow mold that is shaped like the model. The goldsmith then poured molten gold into the mold. Once the metal had hardened, the mold was broken to reveal the object.

The lost wax method of casting metal objects became a highly developed craft in Mesoamerica and elsewhere. Goldsmiths of the Mixtec people, who were conquered by the Aztecs 30 years before the Spanish arrived, produced gold objects that were very precise and realistic. In the region now known as Panama, craftsmen made tiny gold frogs that must be viewed under a magnifying glass to see all of the details.

Objects of gold and silver were cast by a two-stage process. The gold part was cast first, and the silver, which has a lower melting point, was then cast onto the gold.

27

PRECIOUS STONES

The craftsmen of the Andes and Mesoamerica made many beautiful objects using precious stones. The Inca greatly valued the blue-green turquoise, which they worked into objects of gold and silver. The Mesoamericans favored jade—its green color was associated with water and maize, both of which were essential to life.

A STONE-AGE CULTURE

The Mesoamerican civilizations were stone-age cultures. Metals were not widely used for practical purposes by people such as the Aztecs. Although they did have some copper tools, metals such as gold were mostly used for decoration.

Most of the tools used in Mesoamerica were made from stone, such as the glassy volcanic rock called obsidian that they used to make blades. Obsidian blades were used for everything from the ritual killing of sacrificial victims to the preparation of food in the home. The skills of the Aztecs in working and carving stones was second to none.

MAKING MOSAICS

Turquoise, a rare and valuable blue-green mineral, was popular with the Aztecs as well as the Inca. They would grind and polish turquoise to make thin, irregular plates, which they used in mosaics on pendants, masks, and other decorated items. The mosaic pieces were set in place with a variety of glues, such as tree resins and the sap of particular orchids.

Mesoamericans made this turquoise mask (above) to represent the god Quetzalcoatl.

A modern stoneworker prepares gemstones.

This Mayan pendant (below) was carved from jade.

SHAPING STONES

The stoneworkers of the Americas shaped hard stones, such as jade, quartz, amethyst, and turquoise, by grinding with abrasives. The abrasives were quartz or jade that had been crushed and pulverized into different-sized granules—from roughly the size of salt grains to the finest polishing powder, which was as smooth as flour.

The gemstone workers were called lapidaries. They began their work with the coarsest grit for the initial carving and shaping of the stone. As the piece took shape, they used finer and finer abrasives. Eventually, they gave the stone a final, mirror-like polish by applying the polishing powder with a piece of wet cloth or leather.

CUTTING AND DRILLING

Tools for cutting pieces of jade and other hard stones were varied. Stoneworkers used a thin slab of sandstone or an abrasive grit glued (perhaps with rubber) to a piece of wood. Another tool was made from wet strips of leather coated with an abrasive powder that were pulled back and forth in a sawing motion across the stone.

Rotary drills, made from reeds or bone, spun by twirling them between the palms of the craftsman's hands, were also used with grit. The stoneworkers had to drill holes to make beads and pendants, but it must have been extremely slow and hard work.

29

INCA ROADS

The Inca did not invent the wheel and neither did the Aztecs, but they built a remarkable system of roads linking the various parts of their empire. Two main roads ran from north to south, one following the coast and the other following the line of the Andes.

A cobbled alley in Pisac, Peru, starts the Inca Trail to Machu Picchu.

COMMUNICATIONS NETWORK

The roads were the empire's communications network. Ordinary people weren't allowed to use them at all. Messengers, called *chasquis*, ran along the roads carrying messages to and from the capital. They worked like relay runners, one man taking over from another at stone shelters placed along the way. In one day, a chain of runners could carry a message 150 miles (241 km).

Larger rest houses called *tambos* were built beside the roads. These were equipped with food and military supplies for the soldiers of the Inca army who also used the roads.

TWO MAIN ROADS

The most important road was the Andes route, called the Camino Real in Spanish, which ran for more than 3,100 miles (4,989 km). It began in Quito, Ecuador, passed through the capital city Cuzco, and ended in what is now Tucumán, Argentina. At its highest, the Camino Real reached altitudes of more than 16,400 feet (5,000 m). The coastal road, El Camino de la Costa, ran parallel to the sea for about 2,500 miles (4,023 km) and was linked to the Camino Real by many smaller

The Inca constructed rope bridges so they could cross rivers and canyons.

side roads. The coast road was up to 16.5 feet (5 m) wide and lined with mud walls where it passed through irrigated valleys. Fruit trees were planted to give shade. The mountain road was narrower and unwalled. It zigzagged up slopes, and stone steps were cut where it was very steep. Wide causeways paved with flat stones were built where the road crossed marshy ground.

ROPE BRIDGES

Where the roads crossed canyons in the mountains, the Inca built rope suspension bridges that were strong enough for pack animals and travelers on foot.

To make a rope bridge, the Inca placed a pair of heavy stone anchors on either side of the canyon and connected them with strong cables of woven *ichu* grass, which grows widely in the Andes and was also used to thatch roofs. Branches were braided between these cables to form the walking surface of the bridge. Two more cables were put in place as guard rails. The bridges were so heavy that they tended to sag in the middle, and they swayed in high winds. Local villagers were responsible for the upkeep of the bridges, and the cables were replaced annually.

TRAVEL BY WATER

The Inca lived by lakes and rivers in the Andes mountains and by the coast of the Pacific Ocean, taking their fishing boats out to cast their nets, and perhaps to trade far afield. The Aztecs built their capital city on a lake, so they naturally made boats to travel around in.

REED BOATS

In many areas timber was in short supply, so the Inca used a type of reed called *totora* that grew around the lakes. They cut and trimmed the reeds and bound them in tight bundles that were light, strong, and buoyant.

A number of bundles were tied together to form each boat. They were flexible and could be curved to form the pointed bow of the boat, allowing it to slip through the water. People living by Lake Titicaca in Peru still make these reed boats, called *balsas*, today.

Thor Heyerdahl's balsa raft Kon-Tiki *is on display in Oslo, Norway.*

CANALS AND CANOES

Both the Maya and the Aztecs made canoes from hollowed-out tree trunks for traveling along the many waterways in the Valley of Mexico. The Aztec capital of Tenochtitlán was crisscrossed by canals that served as its main passageways. They were often crowded with canoes carrying produce to and from the market. The Aztecs had no wheeled vehicles, so canoes were the most efficient way of bringing goods into the city. Many homes backed onto one of the canals, and many probably had a canoe tied up outside.

DID THE INCAS CROSS THE PACIFIC?

In 1947, the Norwegian explorer Thor Heyerdahl set out to prove his theory that people from South America had settled islands in the South Pacific. In Peru, his team built a raft using balsa wood logs and other materials, such as bamboo and banana leaves,

A mother and her child (left) sit in their reed boat on Lake Titicaca in the Andes.

in traditional Incan style. He called it *Kon-Tiki*, after an old name for the Inca sun god. Heyerdahl and his crew sailed across the Pacific for 101 days, covering nearly 4,350 miles (7,000 km) before running aground in the Tuamotu Islands. Although Heyerdahl's theory was never proved, evidence has emerged recently that trade did take place between South America and islands in the South Pacific before the Spanish arrived.

BOWMEN IN CANOES

Canoes played a part in the defense of Tenochtitlán against the Spaniards. The Spaniards tried to enter the city along one of the causeways that joined the city to the mainland. Aztec bowmen moved swiftly along the canals in their canoes, coming at the Spaniards from both sides of the causeway and firing arrows at them.

KEEPING RECORDS

We see words all the time—in books, magazines, and newspapers and on signs, computer screens, and cell phones. Imagine trying to run a civilization without a written language. The Inca kept no written records, while the Aztecs and Maya had a complex picture writing system.

KNOTTED STRINGS

The Inca recorded information on devices called quipus. Basically, a quipu was a cord from which a number of knotted strings made from alpaca or llama wool or cotton were hung. The arrangement and sizes of the knots tied on these strings held the information. Some quipus have been discovered with more than 2,000 strings, so the information they carried was probably quite complex.

So far as we know, quipus were used to keep records of things bought and sold, tax records, population numbers, and anything else that could be counted. They were also used like calendars to record and keep track of special events.

Some researchers believe that quipu knots may be a system of writing. Some sequences of knots appear to form a code, standing for a place or a person, rather than just a number. The position of different strings and their color might also play a part in the code. No one knows for certain.

These knotted strings are a quipu that was made in Peru between 1430 and 1532.

The Codex Cospi is a kind of calendar that contained information to help the Aztecs predict the future.

TALKING PICTURES

The people of Mesoamerica had a picture writing system, similar to the hieroglyphs of ancient Egypt. The Maya's system was the most fully developed and was composed of many detailed pictures called glyphs. Each glyph stood for a word or a part of a word.

A glyph can be both an idea and a sound. A number was shown as a number or as the god associated with that number.

The Aztecs had a picture language, too, although most Aztecs were illiterate. War was shown by a picture of a shield and a club. Talking was a little scroll coming from someone's mouth. They also had pictures for descriptive names—*Chimalpopoca*, for example, means "smoking shield." The symbols in an Aztec manuscript are not placed one after the other like words in a book. They are like an artistic composition where many things may be going on. Every symbol gives a clue to the reader who has to decipher what is happening.

The glyphs in a Mayan codex are very difficult to decipher.

THE MAYA CODICES

The Maya codices (singular codex) are books written in glyphs on long strips of paper, several yards in length, made from the inner bark of the fig tree. Only four of these codices survive today. Much of what we know about the Maya, such as their knowledge of astronomy, has been learned from the codices.

Marking Time

Societies have always needed a way to mark time. The Egyptians needed to know when the Nile flooded, so they could prepare their fields in time. The Maya believed that it was very important to perform ceremonies on the correct day, in the same way we remember a friend's birthday today. For all of these things you need a calendar.

The Mayan Calendar

The Mayan calendar is very complex, but very accurate. It uses three different systems for calculating dates: the Haab (the civil calendar), the Tzolkin (the divine calendar) and the Long Count. It was adopted by other peoples of Mesoamerica, including the Aztecs, who didn't make changes but replaced the Mayan names for the days and months with their own.

The Haab is divided into 18 months of 20 days each and five extra days, making 365 days in total. The days of the month were

This circular sculpture is thought to be an Aztec calendar stone.

The symbols for each of the 20 days in the Mayan month.

numbered from 0 to 19—the Maya were unique in having a "zero" day. They also knew that a year was 365 and a quarter days long.

THE LONG COUNT

The Long Count was based on a 360-day *tun* (a measure of time, similar to a year) and a number system based on 20. Four hundred *tuns* made a *baktun* of 144,000 days, and 13 *baktuns* equaled a Great Cycle of 5,130 years. The Maya, Aztecs, and other Mesoamerican peoples believed that at the end of each Great Cycle, the world ceases to exist and a new one is created. The current Great Cycle ends on December 23, 2012.

The Maya had two different week lengths: a numbered week of 13 days, and a named week of 20 days. These weeks ran together in a cycle that repeated every 260 days. This was the Tzolkin calendar. Each day had different associations of good and bad luck.

THE CALENDAR ROUND

Together, the Tzolkin and the Haab systems formed a cycle that repeated once every 52 years. This was the Calendar Round. The peoples of Mesoamerica looked on the end of each cycle with trepidation.

The Aztecs celebrated it as the Binding Up of the Years, or the New Fire Ceremony. All fires were allowed to burn out on the last day of the cycle. Then, as the first day of the new cycle began, Aztec priests lit a new sacred fire on the breast of a sacrificial victim. From the flames of this fire the people relit their own fires and began feasting.

MAGIC AND MEDICINE

The peoples of Mesoamerica and the Andes believed that illness was caused by evil magic or punishment by the gods. Therefore, any cure had to be a magical one or brought about by pleasing the god in question. But they also observed which of the magical cures worked and built up a knowledge of medicinal plants.

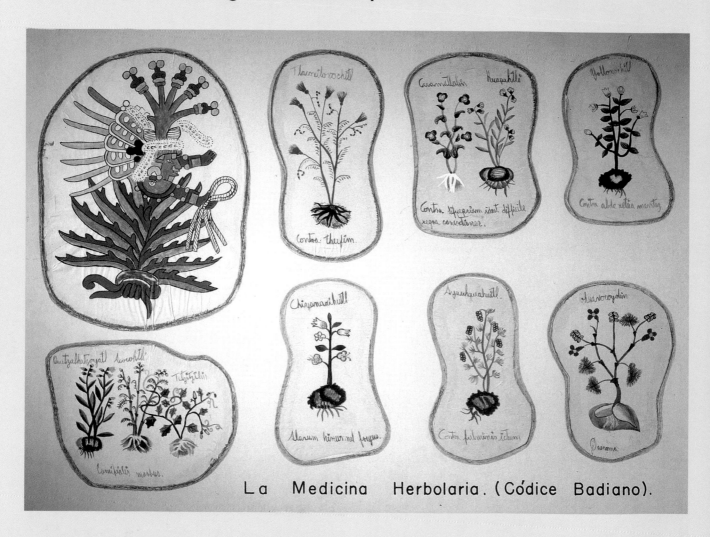

La Medicina Herbolaria. (Códice Badiano).

HERBAL MEDICINE

The Inca often treated people's illnesses and ailments with a variety of herbal remedies, such as the leaves of the tobacco and coca plants. For example, inhaling tobacco powder was thought to clear the head. The leaves of the coca plant were used for relieving pain, increasing alertness, and boosting endurance. The Aztecs grew plants for medicinal use in special gardens. Medicinal seeds and roots were often combined with vanilla or cocoa to make them taste better.

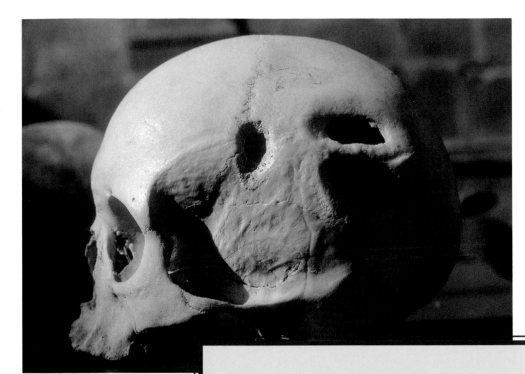

An Inca skull showing evidence of trepanation.

Aztec medical procedures (left), such as treating a fever, were recorded in the Florentine codex (1575–1577).

EARLY SURGERY

The Aztecs and Inca knew a lot about the way the body worked and could treat wounds and broken limbs. They had few medical instruments. Their knives were made of flint or obsidian stone, and they stitched wounds using human hair or vegetable fibers with needles made of human or animal bone.

The treatment for a broken limb was first to press the area of the fracture, stretch the bone to its normal length and position, and then join the broken ends. A poultice made of pulverized plant root was applied, and the limb was held in place with wooden splints bound with cords. Just as doctors today insert metal pins to help hold mending bones together, Aztec surgeons sometimes inserted sticks inside exposed bone fractures.

AZTEC DENTISTRY

The Aztecs took good care of their teeth, rinsing them with water after every meal and shifting food particles with thorns or

OPENING THE SKULL

The Inca performed successful surgery on people's skulls. In a technique we call trepanation, they cut a hole in the skull, probably to relieve pressure on the brain caused by swelling as a result of blows to the head. The patient was given coca leaves to reduce the pain. Some survived this procedure because trepanned skulls have been found that show evidence of healing.

toothpicks. Tartar was removed with charcoal in salted water, or with a mixture of salt, alum, chilli, and cochineal applied using a root as a brush. Swollen and abscessed gums were pierced with thorns and cleaned of pus.

Although the Aztecs frequently drilled their teeth to decorate them with gold and precious stones, there is no evidence that they drilled them to remove decay.

MILITARY TECHNOLOGY

Fighting between rival peoples and city-states was a regular occurrence in Mesoamerica and the Andes. Men of both regions were encouraged to develop a fighting spirit. The Aztecs believed that human sacrifice kept the sun moving through the sky, so their warriors always looked for new victims to capture.

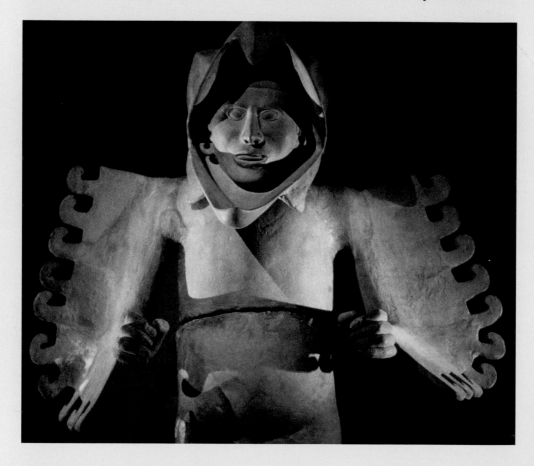

A life-size sculpture of an Aztec eagle warrior.

THE ARMY OF THE INCA

The Inca army was a large, well-disciplined force of men. Every male Inca was required to serve in the army at least once in his life. An Inca soldier's main weapons were a sling, a spear, and a mace or club. The Inca, like the Aztecs, had no bronze or iron for making weapons. The Inca also recruited warriors from the tribes living in the tropical forests, because they were particularly skilled at using bows and arrows and shooting darts from blowpipes. At the start of a battle, the soldiers attacked their opponents from a distance, first using slings and then their bows. When the two forces were close enough, they fought hand to hand with clubs and spears. For protection, Inca soldiers carried shields made of wood or leather.

AZTEC WARRIORS

Aztec warriors were armed with wooden warclubs and spears that had sharp blades made of obsidian, a black, glassy substance.

A spear from a weapon known as an atlatl (pronounced ot-lottle) could be hurled a long distance, more than 300 feet (91 m). The weapon had a wooden shaft with a handle on one end and a groove with a cup at the other end. The butt of the spear fit into the cup. The spear was thrown by flicking the upper arm and wrist forward. The Spanish discovered that a spear from an Aztec's atlatl pierced their armor.

Aztec warriors had shields made of wood or woven maize cane. Often, these were decorated with colorful feathers. They also wore close-fitting body armor made of quilted cotton that helped to soften the blow of an opponent's club. Successful warriors had helmets showing their membership of a warrior order. For example, the members of the Knights of the Eagle wore eagle-head helmets.

The thrower starts to throw an atlatl like a javelin, then halfway through the action, he flicks his arm and wrist forward.

THE SPANISH CONQUEST

Although greatly outnumbered by the armies of the Aztecs, Inca, and other people, the Spanish conquistadors who arrived at the beginning of the sixteenth century won many victories because their technology was superior. They brought harquebuses (an early form of a gun, mounted on a tripod), which shocked and amazed the natives. Aztec and Inca shields and armor of wood and cotton were no match for their steel swords, crossbows, and pikestaffs. The horses and war dogs of the Spaniards were also used to terrifying effect.

Aztec, Inca, and Maya Time Line

ca. 3000 B.C. The first pottery is made in the Americas in what is now Colombia and Ecuador.

ca. 1200 B.C.–400 B.C. The Olmec civilization flourishes in Mexico.

ca. 300 B.C. The beginning of the Mayan civilization in Mesoamerica. Large city-states are formed in Mexico, such as Teotihuácan.

A.D. 100 The decline of the Olmecs.

ca. A.D. 500 The first great Mayan city of Tikal is founded.

ca. A.D. 600 The Mayan civilization is at the height of its powers. An unknown event destroys the city of Teotihuácan.

ca. A.D. 850 The collapse of the powerful Mayan culture.

A.D. 899 The city of Tikal is abandoned.

A.D. 1000 The Chimu culture appears in Peru.

ca. A.D. 1100 The Toltecs build their capital at Tula in Mexico.

ca. A.D. 1200 The Aztecs move into the Valley of Mexico. Manco Cápac becomes the first Sapa Inca (emperor) and founds the Inca Empire.

A.D. 1325 The Aztec city of Tenochtitlán is founded. The Aztecs begin their rise to power in Mexico.

A.D. 1438 The Inca build the fortress of Sacsayhuaman and the city of Machu Picchu.

A.D. 1470 The Inca conquer the Chimu kingdom.

A.D. **1492** Christopher Columbus reaches the Americas, making landfall on the island of Hispaniola in the West Indies, and Europe discovers the New World.

A.D. **1493** The first Spanish settlement is established at Hispaniola. Portugal and Spain agree to divide the New World between them.

A.D. **1498** Columbus discovers the mainland of South America.

A.D. **1517** Spaniards under the command of Fernández de Córdoba arrive in the Yucatan, a part of Mexico. They bring with them diseases such as smallpox, measles, and influenza unknown in the New World. Within a century, Mesoamerica's population will be devastated by these diseases.

A.D. **1519** Hernán Cortés begins the conquest of the Aztec empire.

A.D. **1521** Tenochtitlán is destroyed.

A.D. **1522** Tenochtitlán is rebuilt and renamed Mexico City.

A.D. **1532** Francisco Pizarro begins the conquest of the Incan empire.

A.D. **1572** Tupac Amaru, the last Incan emperor, is captured and executed.

GLOSSARY

abrasive A durable substance used in grinding and polishing.

abscess A painful collection of pus that forms as a result of an infection.

acoustic Relating to sound and hearing.

adobe Sun-dried brick of mud and straw.

alloy A mixture of two or more metals. Bronze is an alloy of copper and tin.

alpaca A South American mammal, similar to a llama, that has silky soft wool.

balsa A boat of reed bundles tied together.

causeway A raised roadway for crossing marshy or swampy ground.

chapines (singular chapin) Blocks of dried mud for growing seedlings on a *chinampa*.

chasqui One of the trained runners who delivered messages along the Inca roads.

chinampa An Aztec system of reclaiming swampy land for planting crops.

chuño A freeze-dried potato product from the high plains of the Andes.

cochineal An insect that lives on cacti that is fried and turned into a red dye.

codex A book written on parchment that is rolled up or folded.

embarro A mixture of red mud and weeds for building traditional Mayan houses.

embossing Decorating a piece of metal with a raised design.

glaze A hard, waterproof coating added to the surface of pottery.

glyph A picture or character that stands for a letter, a sound, or a word.

gum A sticky substance from certain plants.

hieroglyph One of the picture symbols used in the Egyptian system of writing.

huaira An oven for smelting metals.

Huari A civilization that flourished in Peru between A.D. 600 and 1000.

ichu A tough grass from the Andes.

irrigation Supplying land with the water needed to ensure plant growth.

jerky A dried beef snack.

lapidary A craftsman who cuts and polishes precious stones.

masonry Stone or brick structures.

Mesoamerica A region that includes Mexico and Central America.

Mixtec An ancient civilization of skilled metalworkers from Mexico.

Moche A civilization that flourished in Peru between A.D. 100 and 800.

mortar A mixture of sand, cement, and water for holding masonry blocks together.

obsidian A volcanic glass that can be turned into sharp-edged weapons and tools.

Olmec A great Mexican civilization that flourished from 1200 B.C. to 400 B.C.

polygonal Having many sides.

poultice A moist plant pulp applied to wounds to reduce inflammation and aid healing.

pyramid A large building with a square base and four triangular sides rising to a point.

quilted Made of stitched layers of fabric.

quipu A series of knotted strings that the Inca used for keeping records.

raising A technique for hammering a sheet of metal into a bowl.

sling A looped strap used to whirl and throw a small projectile such as a stone.

smelting Extracting metal from its ore by heating and melting.

splint A device for immobilizing and supporting a broken bone while it heals.

talud-tablero A style of architecture in which a platform (the *tablero*) rests on top of a sloping wall (the *talud*).

tamales A steamed maize parcel stuffed with meat or vegetable fillings.

tambo A rest house on an Inca road where travelers found food and lodging.

Toltecs Warrior and trading people who lived in Mesoamerica from A.D. 900 to 1200.

Totonacs A people who lived in eastern Mexico at the time of the Spanish conquest.

tumbaga An alloy of copper and gold.

turquoise A blue-green, semi-precious stone that was highly prized by the Aztecs.

vicuña A South American mammal, similar to a llama, that is prized for its wool.

FURTHER READING

Bingham, Jane. *The Inca Empire.* Chicago, Ill.: Raintree, 2007.

Morris, Ting. *Arts and Crafts of the Aztecs and Maya.* North Mankato, Minn.: Smart Apple Media, 2007.

WEB SITES FOR STUDENTS

http://coe.fgcu.edu/students/webb/meso/maya.htm
Learn more about the life of the Maya and their religion, food, architecture, and more.

http://library.thinkquest.org/27981/
This site provides more information about the everyday life of the Aztecs.

http://www.42explore2.com/inca.htm
Uncover more about the Incas at this site that has project ideas and links to many other helpful Web sites.

WEB SITES FOR TEACHERS

http://school.discoveryeducation.com/lessonplans/programs/conquestamericas/
Visit this Web site for a fun lesson plan about the "Conquest of the Americas."

http://webexhibits.org/calendars/calendar-mayan.html
This site explains the calendar of the Maya.

Index